Cornelius GURLITT

SCHOOL OF VELOCITY FOR BEGINNERS
Opus 141

FOR PIANO

K 03496

School of Velocity

for

Beginners.

C. GURLITT. Op. 141.

Moderato.
2.
f

Con moto.
3.
mf
cantabile.
f

Allegretto.
4.
mf
f

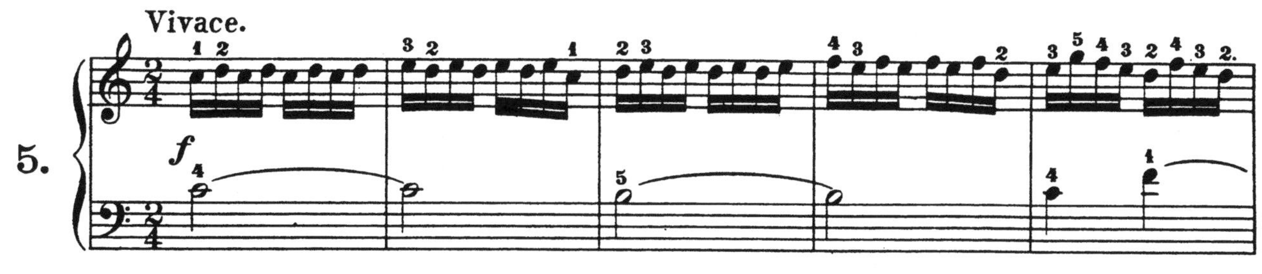
Vivace.
5.
f

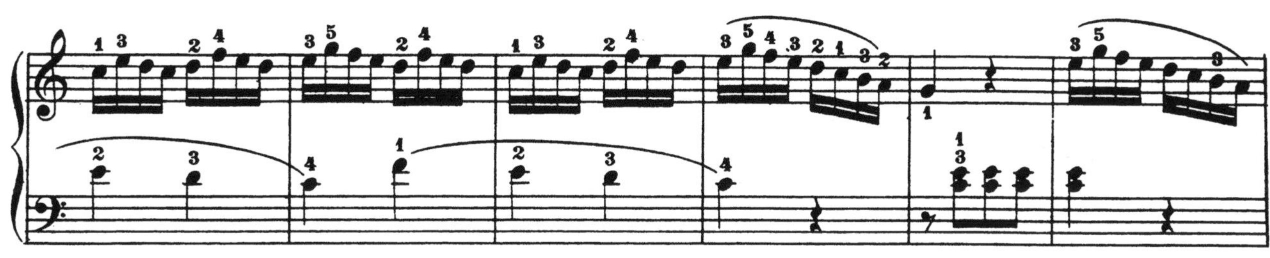

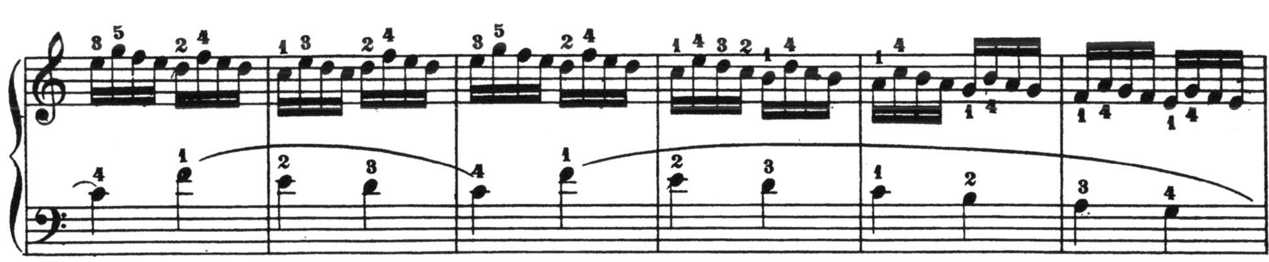

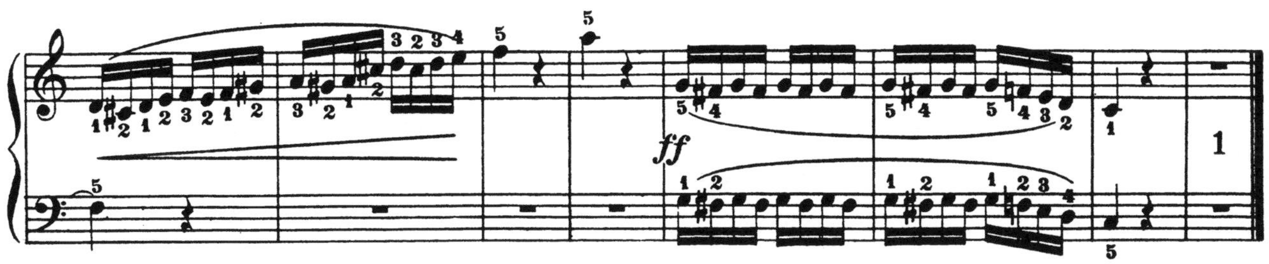
ff

8
Vivace.
6.
f
cresc.
cresc.
ff

Moderato.
7.
p
mf
f
3496

Moderato.
8.
p sosten.
espress.
f
decresc.
p

Allegretto.
9.
mf
cresc.
f
dim.
p con anima.
decresc.
dolce
dim.
p
decresc.

Allegro.
10.
ff

Allegretto.
11.
mf scherz.
cresc.
f
decresc.
pp

Allegro molto.

Vivace.
13.
mf
f
f
ff

Allegro.
14.
f risoluto.
mf
cresc. molto.
ff
ff

Moderato.
15.
f
marcato molto.
ff
ff

Con moto.
16.
p
mf
p

Andantino.
17.
p con espress.
cresc.
dim.
p
per - den - do - si.
pp

Allegretto.
18.
mf scherz.
f
f
p sosten.
mf
f
mf
f
ff

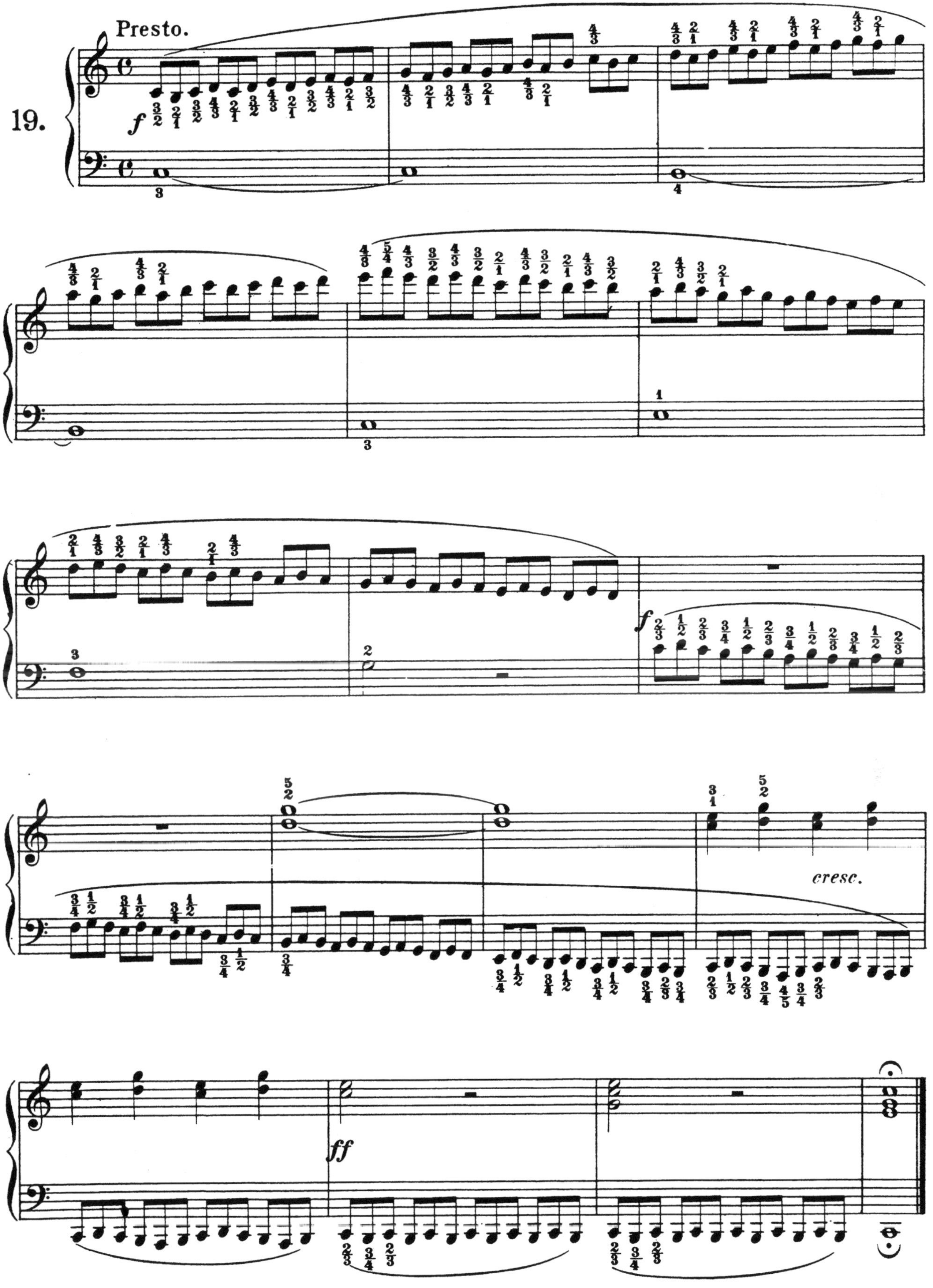
Presto.
19.
f
cresc.
ff

Allegro.
20.
mf

Con moto.
21.
f
f
cresc.
ff

Vivace.
22.
f
cresc.
ff
ff
ff

Moderato.
23.
p espressivo e tenuto il canto.
cresc.
decresc.
cresc.
poco riten.
p a tempo.
cresc.
cresc. p

Molto vivace.
24.
f
risoluto.